18 wheels and a Roll of foil over the Road and eating Well

By: Brian Windham

About this Book

Sometimes Lessons learned in life make some of the best reference manuals to be read. After Traveling for work both as an over the road truck driver delivering to some of the most remote regions in the united states and also as a Contractor working both in and out of *state, there were many nights I would get to the hotel too late to find anything to eat other than snacks from a gas station. With that being said, I searched for a solution to this annoying problem and also realized that there was no need to "grab fast food on the fly anymore. Many might wince at my solution here, but I put together a mini Kitchen toolkit to travel with me using the heat of the cars engine as my Cooking medium. Now before you click off of this book thinking **"Gross"** or **"How Odd"** I want to tell you rest assured that none of my meals have ever tasted like gasoline or oil. Tinfoil effectively seals foods to keep odd smells out and does not allow juices to leak out. At 10 O clock at night, I would prefer a pork tenderloin over a cheeseburger any-day. Follow along as I am happy to share my technique with* *you including sharing some of my best recipes*

Chapters -

Chapter I – Building the toolbox things to have with you

Chapter II – Ingredients to Carry with you for your traveling kitchen

Chapter I -

When you travel I think we are all guilty of the Mindset of traveling light, meaning not several Bags to bring with, but in order to adapt to the technique in this book, I recommend getting a small to medium sized tote to keep with you when you travel so you will have your traveling kitchen no matter where you go. So to get started lets get some tools gathered up

first, a tote to keep items out of the way-while traveling

Tin Foil, needed is not a tiny roll but a fairly decent sized roll you will use a fair amount with your recipes, think of foil as your dutch Oven

BBQ utensils – Grabbing your meal package wrapped in foil is going to be hot, using the tongs saves fingers and the fork that comes with is handy to hold meats while you slice

Can Opener- *a must have in the tool lit, I actually prefer a can opener with the bottle cap remover and point to puncture a can*

Metal Coffee cup *- for Cooking*

Cutting Board -

both preparing and cutting up meats require a good clean cutting board. Find a cutting board that fits in the tote you are loading. When I purchased my tote I gathered everything I needed to put inside before I purchased the tote.

Gallon sized zip-lock bags - *Always put your sauces and seasonings in a zip lock to-keep the tote clean and dry. Bags can be washed out and they are great to put back into your cooler.*

Plastic Plates and Utensils -
I carry a setting for two people in my mess kit. Plastic works best and is more durable when you travel.

Travel Sized dish detergent -
To sterilize your dishes and cutlery dawn dish soap does wonders. Doesn't hurt to bring a pot scrubber along with.

Large Knives -
I highly recommend carrying two knives in your tote to cook with, from a sanitary perspective one knife for slicing meats and the second knife for slicing your breads. Having one knife is more work especially if someone you are feeding wanted a second slice of bread.

** Tech Tip – Reaching into a tote at nighttime can be downright dangerous especially with sharp* *knives in the tote. What works well to cover the knives is empty paper towel cardboard tubes. I have foam inserted into both of my tubes so the knife stays on the tube (Always clean knives first)..*

Food thermometer-

If cooking roasts or larger meats its a smart move to check internal temperatures before serving temps are below;

Eggs and all ground meats must be cooked to 160°F

poultry and fowl to 165°F

fresh meat steaks, chops and roasts to 145°F

Egg dishes (such as frittata, quiche) 160°F

Leftovers and casseroles
165°F

Food should always be prepared as follows, tear a bottom sheet of foil large enough to cover the meal being cooked. *Adding all the seasonings to the meat,* **put a top sheet over the meal and carefully wrap the foil under the bottom sheet making a lip to prevent spillage or leakages into the engine surface.** Note ** **Some marinade is OK but engine cooking is not good for something such as Stews or soups on a passenger car.**

If Operating a tractor trailer soups and stews are possible and I will discuss later in the book the next chapter is devoted to gathering seasonings and vegetables

Chapter II -

I understand this whole concept seems strange or odd to most, and it takes practice to get it down. My seasonings and spices I was changing and adding to for almost 6 months before having everything I needed. Below I am sharing with you whats in my tote. Again, large zip-lock bags are your friend here. Also don't overlook the dollar-store for seasonings for your mess kit, it's an economical way to be well stocked.

Iodized salt

Black Pepper

Lemon Pepper

Red Pepper

Garlic Salt

Onion Flakes

Dried instant onion soup
(for Meats)

Chives

Allspice

Soy Sauce

Misc. from restaurants you stop at on occasion. The neat little margarine packages, sugar packets and salt and pepper packets are always handy to have on the fly. I keep about one-dozen of each on hand

Chapter III -

After gathering tools and spices, the next step is to survey your engine to **observe the best cooking points for your foil food packages.** Things to keep in *mind are to be cautious of moving parts and the associated dangers.* **Preparing food to cook on an engine simply means to cut the food to size to tuck it into the designated areas so, if cooking a pork tenderloin instead of leaving the cut of meat long, cut it into third's or even quarters to fit safely into the nooks and crannies. Things to watch out for include fan blades, that will chop your package into an unusable mess, Fan belts, which the packages can get caught in and stuck under the throttle cable causing an unwanted stuck gas pedal.**

By no means am I trying to discourage cooking on the car engine cooking, however it's important to know the right and wrong areas to place the packages. **Meats need to be in the hottest points of the engine** *where* **vegetables cook perfectly** *in cooler locations on the engine.* Plastics have really no thermal heat transfer value so **I recommend always finding metal surfaces to lay packages on.** Areas I really like are the **top of the intake manifolds, the space between the water pump and engine block, if front wheel drive, there are great cook points on the back of the engine by the transmission and basically anywhere you can get a good heat transfer.** For safety, you can use bailing wire to hold the foil packages in place but never tie it to any car wiring, or the throttle linkage. Instead look for brackets like power steering and alternator brackets.

Cook times vary by meat and this is a quick, handy guide to keep in mind as far as when to turn your dishes and how many miles are needed to cook.

Sliced, peeled potatoes: 55 miles

Shrimp: 30-50 miles

Trout or Salmon: 60-100 miles

Chicken breasts: 60 miles at 65 mph

Chicken wings: 140-200 miles

Pork tenderloin: 250 miles

Preparing your meal-

Foil is about to become your new best friend. Grab a sheet of foil large enough to comfortably cover the food/ingredients. You don't want to be cheap on foil here, more is better. Wrap the foil around, creating a package, and crimp the foil tightly. You want a seal all around the food. And then do it again. And then again. Triple-wrapping in foil is the only way to ensure a tight, sealed, safe package. Recipes in the following pages are recipes I had written down in a notebook and I've used them many times Over the Years. Feel Free to modify them as you see fit and please share them with others interested in this new style of cooking, it's not only fun, but it's a more healthy alternative to fast food dinners that may not digest properly.

Bonn Appetite!

Chapter IV -

The recipe Collection below is for the main coarse only. Some recipes are well complicated with a slice of bread and butter. It's recommended to pick up a couple of Loaves of bread *before the trip to have with you. Bottled water is always good to bring along as well. Here are my recipe's*

Travelers Tenderloin
Ingredients:

1 large pork tenderloin, butterflied

½ Cup of french dressing

1 envelope Lipton's french onion soup (leave dry)

1 clove of garlic minced

light Coating of Salt and pepper on inside and out

Blend together all of the ingredients (except the pork) Cut pork tenderloin in half and butterfly. and spread across the inside of both pieces of pork tenderloin. Close up the pork, and smear remaining ingredients over the top.

Triple-wrap in foil and place on a medium-hot part of the engine. Turn once (125 miles) during cooking.

***if your trip is less than 250 miles the variation is to pre cook the tenderloin before leaving on your trip providing you have Oven access**

Shrimp of the Bayou

Ingredients:

1 pound large shrimp

6 small jalapeno peppers

2 cloves garlic Minced

1 medium white onion, finely chopped

Butter or spread

Salt & pepper

Remove seeds from peppers (ouch, they are hot) and mince with the onion and garlic. Butter your foil, add the shrimp and cover with your spicy mixture. Sprinkle a little salt and pepper, then triple-wrap and place in a medium part of the engine. Delicious, seasoned, spicy shrimp await. Cooking distance: 40-45 Miles.

Rice Pilaf is excellent with the shrimp making it a very filling meal. Grocery stores now carry rice pilaf in a microwavable bag, so when cooking this I throw a package or two on the engine next to the shrimp and in Under an hour dinner is ready

Double clutch Potatoes

Ingredients:

1/2 pound Russet potatoes

1 cup milk

1 cup water

2 ounces grated (Tillamook cheddar cheese)

¼ Cup chopped white onion

Butter

Salt & pepper

Peel and slice potatoes to 1.4 inch thick. Place in a saucepan with the milk and water and simmer 10 minutes. Drain, then spread onto Foil Covered with generous butter. Sprinkle with your cheese) and Onions. Sprinkle with butter, triple-wrap and place around medium-hot parts of the engine. Delicious. Cook Distance 55 Miles

Simple Chicken

1 standard sized turkey breast (or 2 chicken breasts)

*1/8 tsp salt, or to taste
1 tsp lemon pepper
seasoning
1 tsp oil or butter*

*Place your turkey or
chicken on buttered foil.
Sprinkle the seasonings on
each side. Seal the foil as
described above and place
on the hot spot on your
motor. Allow to cook 45
minutes if sitting still or an
hour if driving. Check
internal temperature using
a food thermometer. It
needs to be 165 degrees at
the center to ensure that all
bacteria are dead. Cook
Distance 65-70 Miles*

For more flavoring add onion to the recipe or if you prefer it zesty try adding a rub to the chicken.

Beef fajitas on the fly

Ingredients:

black beans – 1 can

small flower tortillas – 1 pkg

round steak cut into strips – ½ Lb, *soaked in marinade inside a zip-lock bag round steak should be thin variety*

Sauteed onion – 1 Large
onion in strips

Bell Pepper Strips – Cut
just like Onion, Combine
with onion strips drizzle
with oil and twist foil shut
to cook.

Shredded Cheese Package
– Keep in Cooler

**Tearing a sheet of foil,
strain a can of black
beans and add to the
center of foil. Add some
leaves of Cilantro to the
top of the beans. Pull the
edges of foil upward
careful not spilling the
beans. Twist the top shut
then add on top of
another sheet of foil. In a
separate Package, place
the meat strips lengthwise
and add a little bit of**

marinade to the meat to keep from drying out. Add the other two packages on the engine.

Total cook-time should be about an hour and 15 minutes or approximately about 80 Miles. If you prefer tortillas warm, wrap in foil and put on engine for the last 20 miles of the journey. When removing because the meal is in multiple packages, oven mitts and a platter are recommended. Don t forget your cheese and sour cream that are in the

*Cooler either. This dish is
a great feast at the end of
your day. Enjoy.*

Chicken fajitas on the fly

Ingredients:

black beans – 1 can

small flower tortillas – 1 pkg

Chicken breast cut into strips – ½ **Lb,** *soaked in marinade inside a zip-lock bag cut in small strips and soaked in marinade*

Sauteed onion – 1 Large *onion in strips*

Bell Pepper Strips – Cut *just like Onion, Combine with onion strips drizzle*

*with oil and twist foil shut
to cook.*

**Shredded Cheese Package
– Keep in Cooler**

**Tearing a sheet of foil,
strain a can of black
beans and add to the
center of foil. Add some
leaves of Cilantro to the
top of the beans. Pull the
edges of foil upward
careful not spilling the
beans. Twist the top shut
then add on top of
another sheet of foil. In a
separate Package, place
the meat strips lengthwise
and add a little bit of
marinade to the meat to
keep from drying out. Add
the other two packages on
the engine.**

Total cook-time should be about an hour and 15 minutes or approximately about 80 Miles. If you prefer tortillas warm, wrap in foil and put on engine for the last 20 miles of the journey. When removing because the meal is in multiple packages, oven mitts and a platter are recommended. Don't forget your cheese and sour cream that are in the Cooler either. This dish is a great feast at the end of your day. Enjoy.

Manifold
Biscuits

Ingredients:

Empty Soup cans –
depending on family Size,
One can will make two
biscuits. Clean empty soup
cans, removing labels on
them. One can will Make
two biscuits.

Package of twist biscuits
(Fresh dough) Usually found
near the cheese Isle.
Important to get the right
size biscuits that fit the can.

Margarine packets –
Possibly picked up at fast
food restaurant

Jelly Packets – Optional in
Various Flavors

**Preparation- Crack
biscuits opened, prepare
the clean soup can by
tearing a small foil square**

no larger then the diameter of the soup can, spray with non stick cooking spray and place a small uncooked biscuit on the foil. Prepare another piece of foil the same way. Place second biscuit on top. Cover the top of the can with a generous piece if foil and place in direct contact with metal on either intake or exhaust manifold. *Cook distance about 45-60 Miles*

Steamed Spuds

Sometimes the taste of a baked potato is second next

to none. A great meal when traveling in the winter there are many variations, this is my variation.

Ingredients:

Russet potatoes Large- One per Person

Olive oil drizzled on outside of potato

Kosher salt, rub on outside

Iodized salt – flavor to taste

1 dollop of sour cream per potato after Cooking split potato opened mash inside, add butter and sour cream.

*** Optional brown ground beef before trip and keeping cooler to add as a protein.**

To prepare the potatoes clean under tap water, with a fork poke steam holes in potato on both ends. coat with olive oil drizzle with salt and triple wrap in foil. Cooking distance- 150-200 miles. Turn over potatoes at 80 Miles

Flat stack flapjacks

Not really cooking but rewarming previously cooked pancakes with a twist. Mix the pancake mix prior to your trip in the normal size. The twist is because on the open road

there is not time to cook a
three coarse breakfast, I
infuse my Pancakes with
either berries or meats.
For berry pancakes I use
blueberries. For 2 servings
I add ½ cup of blueberries
and cook them in. for a
more hearty variety,
Brown and crumble
breakfast sausage end
add to the batter. Freeze
in tinfoil packages of four

preparation -

Carefully place the
flapjacks either on the
intake manifold or exhaust
manifold. Perfect to put on
engine lock the car and
use remote start from
motel room. After you
load your suitcase pull

package and check. If still cold add 15 miles then pullover and check.

Golden Arches Breakfast of champions

Ingredients:

1 egg *per person*

sliced Kraft cheese *from the cooler- 1 slice per person*

1 English Muffln *per person*

cooking spray – spray bottom of metal camping coffee cup.

Planning ahead, call the Hotel you have reservations at, to see if they offer a continental breakfast. il they do take advantage of their toaster and use one of the offered muffins, **toast without butter and wrap up to take with. Low toaster setting so you don't burn your muffin** Taking your metal coffee cup, spray cooking spray in the bottom. crack egg and add to cup. Whip egg-with your cutlery from your kit. Cover the top with foil, then pop your hood and find a safe place to put the cup so it doesn't keep hood opened but is on hot surface. This cooks quick so I would start car and check in 10-15 minutes. After solid, break loose with spoon, carefully pour onto bottom of muffin, add cheese on top and add the top of muffin. ***Note- if you are not staying at a motel or driving for a one day trip, toast your muffin before starting out.**

GARLIC SHRIMP

Ingredients:

Butter

1/4 pound medium-size raw tiger shrimp in the shell

1 garlic clove, minced

1/2 lemon

Salt, to taste

Prepare 2 squares of heavy-
duty aluminum foil. Butter
the dull sides of each square
almost to the edges.

Rinse the shrimp and divide
them between the squares.
Sprinkle the garlic over the
shrimp, then squeeze lemon
juice over them. Season with
salt.

Wrap the foil tightly around
each shrimp bundle. Tuck
each bundle against the
manifold

Drive 35 miles at 65 mph,
or until the shrimp are
completely pink.

Chicken with a Kick

Ingredients:

2 teaspoons olive oil

1/2 boneless, skinless chicken breast

Salt, to taste

Fresh cilantro

White Onion (Minced)

a few strips of bell pepper, any color or combination

Place (1) teaspoon of the olive oil on the dull side of foil sheets and coat the entire Sheet

*Cut the chicken into 2"
Pieces. Divide the Pieces
between the foil squares.
Season with salt. Snip
cilantro to taste over the
chicken. Divide the pepper
strips over the chicken and
add minced white Onion.
Cooking requires 60 miles
at 65 mph, or until the
chicken is no longer pink.*

**Divided in two this makes
two hearty Portions**

Soups chili and all things Canned

Above we have discussed delicious recipes. There are so many Variations In what can be Cooked on the engine. **It's possible to also cook or warm food from a Can. It requires being put in a warmer spot if it's a stew, soup or dense liquid. I personally prefer the exhaust Manifold for the heating source.** Using Bailing wire and a wire cutter in the car I **cut a 12" piece of wire, peel the paper label off the can and holding the can against the manifold run the wire around it to secure the can.**

This takes some practice to do but its a great way to warm a can of peas, corn or soup for your meal. **Always use a MIT when removing cans and leave the wire long enough to be able to**

untie without getting burned. when opening the can hold it with the MIT on your Hand to avoid burns. Since soup is condensed on nights I had planned Soups I pour boiling hot water in the thermos to have warm water to blend with the soup so its not so thick **(Condensed)**

Comfort foods for the Kiddos-

Hot dogs are certainly a food that will not be argued when out on the road. Small Children can be crabby while traveling so here's *one easy to prepare and guaranteed to please. Combined with Mac and cheese its perfect here's how it's done*

Ingredients-

(1) Package Hot-dog Buns

(1) Box of velveta Mac and cheese

(2) Jumbo Soup Cans

(2) Bottles of bottled water

(1) Spoon for mixing mac and Cheese

Misc Packets Mustard and ketchup free from fast foods

Preparation-

Taking (2) Clean jumbo Soup Cans from your tool Kit, Open a bottled water and fill both cans between

½ and ¾ full of water. Open the box of Mac and Cheese and divide pasta between two Cans, Pour in the water. Cover cans with tinfoil. Next attach Cans

to extremely hot spots on the engine. I like the exhaust Manifolds. take a couple of hot dogs, and maybe a couple of Brats in a foil pouch. Since meats have been pre cooked place the pouch under air cleaner on the intake manifold. Note- it takes water approximately 15 minutes on a stove-top to boil, and water needs to boil for about 7-10 minutes to cook pasta, drive 40 Minutes, pull off the road and peel foil back and test pasta. If Pasta is soft, remove cans,

if not quite cooked give it
15 more miles. After
Cooked, using the spoon
carefully drain water from
can without loosing pasta.
Remove the meat pouch
and set aside. Next stir in
the Cheese Package in
each Can and Mix in. get
buns and condiments out,
dish up macaroni and you
have made another
successful Meal.

Chapter V -

A meal wouldn't be Complete without some sort of sweets for your palate I have developed my own deserts to cook over an engine so the key tools here are listed below assuming you are going to prep in the middle of your trip. **Items below are what's needed to successfully Bake on your engine**

Small plastic mixing bowl

wooden spoon

Paper Baking Cups

Jiffy Cake mixes

Large Metal Cans =Jumbo Sized from Soups

Tinfoil

For starters The Soup Cans Should be Over-sized or Jumbo sized. Each Soup can will hold one baking Cup filled with Cake batter and Covered with foil to keep cupcake clean. Cooking the desert should be parked an at an Idle, Since aluminum foil tears easily. Keeping things clean on the go, these cupcakes are to be served without frosting. Lets get started.

Cupcakes-

For a Family of three for desert

*in a plastic mixing bowl
mix cake mix, egg and
whatever other
ingredients the mix calls
for. After mixed, grab
your Oversize Soup Cans,
place (1) paper baking
Cup in the bottom of each
can. Carefully spoon the
batter into each paper
cup, do not overfill the
Cups.* Next with cups full,
cover the top of the Can
with tinfoil and attach to
the side of exhaust
manifolds. every car is
different so run the
engine for 15-20 minutes
and check. Use a knife or
toothpick to see if batter is
done. When Baked use the
Mitt to remove the can and
serve cupcakes

After a long day, these
cupcakes go good with hot

*chocolate or a cup of coffee.
If your family is bigger see
my next Desert be creative
give it your own spin.*

Coffee
Can Cake-

*One of my personal
Favorites, this does not
come out perfect but
camping or out on the road
its fantastic. It will require
some mileage to cook so
allow between 75-100 miles*

to Bake. If it's in the middle
of summer check more
often.

Ingredients-

(1) Clean 3Lb Coffee Can

**(1) Box of Duncan and
Hines cake Mix**

eggs

Vegetable Oil

Water

In a mixing bowl, Mix all
ingredients removing all
lumps from the Batter. Take
cooking spray and coat the
inside of the coffee can next
pour the cake batter into
the coffee can, but first
make sure there is enough
room to close the hood.

Cover the Can with foil and attach to the exhaust manifold or a good warm area.

Because of the shape of the Cake I would recommend between 80-150 miles before checking the batter. On a tractor trailer I highly recommend the exhaust stacks as a heat source, just make sure can is Covered with good thick foil. Cakes take practice so expect to try this once or twice to perfect the technique. Under no circumstances put the plastic lid on while baking, the plastic will melt. Using the lid to cover the cake after the can cools works great. if your coffee can has a paper lid on it, peel it before baking with it. Metal cans are getting hard to come by so if you cannot find a metal coffee can something else similar sized will work.

Conclusion-

Thank you for reading this. I hope that this has opened a new world for your family. While it may not be for some, it's a much healthier alternative to fast foods and frequent bathroom stops. Engine cooking is an art that takes practice. The big thing to remember is to always use a thick, quality foil for your meals and never try to make a liquid based dish such as a soup or stew. Liquids leak out over your engine and after baked into the engines surfaces will burn and leave a very unpleasant odor in the cockpit. Experiment, and make your own recipes. The thing to remember is that cooking on an engine steams the meal doesn't bake it or fry it so it will be a different Color. When Cooking meats always cut them small or into multiple pieces. Bringing a Cooler is necessary and make sure to brink zip-locks for food storage. With ice in cooler your foods will keep. I hope you enjoy the art of internal Combustion Cooking. Eat well while traveling